iridescent soul

by ayana solarin

CHAPTERS

chapter one

luminescent

it's not easy for me
to look back on our story
and see a precise
beginning or ending

it just kind of happened

but sometimes
the best stories
are the ones
you don't see coming

-a journey back in time

find someone
who looks at you
and loves what they see
without wanting to change
you

-as you are

if we could all
manage
to love each other
just a little bit

the world
would get brighter
every day

-brighter world

in the darkest
of times
draw closer
to your loved ones

let their love
bring light
into your life

-love & light

the memories of us
trap me
like quicksand

*-sometimes i fear i will never
escape*

stop holding on
to people
who don't deserve
your effort

-effort

the golden times
do not shine
while you are in them

they only shine
when you look back at them
and there's
something beautiful
about that

-golden times

self love
is peeling back
all the protective layers
you built around your heart
to hold back
the pain
of all the ways
life has hurt you

-protective layers

life is too short
to be passive

be the kind of person
who dumps the coffee
down the drain
if it isn't good enough
instead of drinking it

don't accept what life gives
you

-demand better

i only hope
that after i cry
my last tear for you
i will look at everything
we gained and lost
together

and think that somehow
it was all worth it

-not everything is meant to
last forever

at rock bottom
looking for a taste of love
in a one night stand

-one night stand

this will be the generation
that finally begins
to listen
to women

-our perspective

life without you
is a desert
without rain

-i thirst

do not give your energy
to those
who take from you
without giving back

-love yourself first

sometimes
you can hate someone
so much

that you miss them

-*complicated endings*

the way you look at me

i would give anything
to feel that again

-love me

when will
the night
end?

sometimes
it feels
like it will go on
forever

-endless night

don't be afraid
to realize
that you have outgrown
certain people
in your life

-move on

things will always get better

hold on to hope
and don't give up

-*things get better*

taking your love
away from me
was the cruelest thing
you could ever do

-*take away*

i need you
in my life

without you
i am incomplete

-incomplete

i hope one day
you smile happily
realizing
you got everything
you ever wanted

-one day

some things
aren't meant
to last forever

smell the rose
while it still lives
but do not hate it
for wilting

that is just
how it was meant
to be

-*temporary roses*

people will think
what they want to
about you
regardless of what
you do about it

so it's better to sit back
and just live your life

-*you will win in the end*

it's easy to feel powerless
as we see
how life rushes by
and our cherished moments
scatter in the breeze

like dust
in the wind

-dust in the wind

the most important thing
in life
is to keep holding on
to your belief
that everything
will work out
in the end

-hold on

chapter two

polychromatic

i remember being a small
child

and thinking
that the cracks between the
sidewalks

could swallow me whole

now the world
doesn't seem so big
as it used too

-*small world*

if i touch
even one soul
with my words
i will consider it
all
worth it

-*worth it*

you deserve someone
who says beautiful things
to you
and means it

and not just
to get things from you

-real

if i could go back in time
and feel the way
you ripped me open
one more time

i would do it

not because of the pain
but because of the way
i began to become
more and more of myself
since that day

-*back in time*

we are all just
broken people

seeking beauty
to help us feel whole

-feel whole

death hangs over our heads
but life
just seems to escape
our notice

-life

the past is dead
the present is alive

do not give the past
any more of your time
than it has already taken

-the past

fire
is not a strong enough word
to describe
what i felt
between the two of us

-fire

there will always be a reason
not to follow your dreams

but there will never be a time
like the present
to pursue them

-follow your dreams

liking sex
doesn't make you
a slut

-change society

our love
cracked open
the cloudy skies
and brought happiness
out of the darkest days

-our love

i found your shirt
under my bed

it still smelled like you

oh, the pain i could have
avoided
if i just had the self control
to throw it away
instead of using it
as an excuse
to talk to you again

-*excuse*

why is it so hard
to let go
of things
that clearly
are no good for you?

-so hard

love is chaos
love is peace

love hurts
love heals
love lives
and love dies

love
is the best part
of being alive

-best part of being alive

no matter how much
you hurt me

i will never stop missing
what we had

-beauty and pain

i miss the innocence
of times past

-nostalgia

forgive those who hurt you

no, not for their sake

but for your own;

because forgiveness
is the first step
to freedom

-forgivness

some people
just need to feel control

just realize
that it has nothing to do with
you
and is only about
their own flaws

-*control freak*

you are the only one
who truly
deserves
you

-*you*

i wish i could convince you
to see yourself
the way i see you

beautiful, perfect
every smile
full of magic

-full of magic

when exactly
did our love
turn to pain?

-*pain*

fire hurts
but sometimes
it's just what we need
to close a wound

-close a wound

i would prefer an open enemy
to a fake friend
like you

-snake

there is always a way out

even when it seems
like the darkness
will never end

-end

i wish i could give you
the love of someone
who had never been betrayed
or lied to
or abused

but that's not who i am
so if you want to love me
you have to realize
you are loving someone
in multiple pieces

-shattered heart

chapter three

luminous

i wish i could stop
blaming myself
for everything that happened

i gave you everything

what else could i have done?

-nothing left

sometimes
you can't be
yourself
until you let go
of someone else

-truth

you deserve a relationship
where you never have to
question
their loyalty

-expect loyalty

your silence
hurt me
worse
than a gunshot

-*silence*

where does your mind
wander
as you look up
at the stars?

i wish i could see
into your mind
and join you
in your daydreams

-daydreams

life
is the art
of rolling with the punches

of bending without breaking
and flying without falling

-life

i wish
i could give you
everything you need
to bloom

-bloom

once you learn
to truly love yourself
there is nothing
anyone else
can truly take away
from you

-*unbreakable*

at some point
you just have to accept
that the only one
who will look after
your best interests
is yourself

-yourself

be careful
who you allow
into your heart

some people disguise harm
as love
like the trojans
sending in destruction
disguised as a gift

-some people send hatred
disguised as love

some people
are just addicted
to leaving

-leaving

you have the strength
deep inside you
to bloom
in a hurricane

-bloom in a hurricane

i would rather wake up
seeing you
than see a sunrise

-you are a sunrise

be wary of those
who see
gentleness
as weakness

-they will only cause you pain

do not waste your love
on those
who do not know
its value

-value

the hardest part
about breaking up
wasn't the heartbreak

it was never knowing why
i wasn't enough
for you

-unanswered questions

deep down inside
we are all
just broken hearted souls
desperate
to feel loved

-deep down

sometimes it feels
like you are holding up
the sky itself
as it crumbles down
around you

-stay strong

there is nothing
more powerful
than a woman
who has truly
fallen in love
with herself

-powerful

i am not proud
of the number of times
i asked you to stay
knowing
it was only a matter of time
before you left
for good

*-i should have realized it was
over*

do not make fun of me
for the way i flinch
when you raise your fist

my abuse
is nothing
to laugh about

-your ignorance hurts me

it's hard to accept
that no matter
how long
you build something
together

in only an instant
it can all come
crashing down
in flames

-catastrophe

i wish i could have sat there
without crying
when you told me
it was over

i wish i could have stolen
the satisfaction
of victory
from beneath you

-i still hate you for the way
you left

despite your struggle
to accept it

know that you
are beautiful
and nothing
can change that

-you are beautiful

chapter four

iridescent

the funny thing
about the stars
is that when we watch them
from our perspective
it seems as if
they never move
and yet
we know
that they do

in the same way
life changes
sometimes so slowly
that we don't notice
and by the time
we do

everything
has changed
under our noses

-change

you said
you were ready
for the fire
and yet
you flinched
when you touched me

-liar

do not ever
let anyone
tell you
you are too much
for them

-too much

why does it feel
like everyone leaves me
eventually

-everyone leaves me

i miss
the way it felt
to not know
how it felt
to have
your heart broken

-the world didn't hurt

i know
we don't have
too much time left
together

just sit with me
and let's enjoy
one last moment
of love
together

-one last moment

don't give your time
to those
who could never love you
the way
you deserve
to be loved

-don't waste your time

don't be afraid
to let go
of the things
that hold you back

-let go

i wish it could have been
as easy for me
to walk away
as it was for you

-it hurts me that it didn't hurt
you

do not give your heart
to someone
who does not see you
as an equal

-equal footing

it was so much easier
to start new relationships
back when heartbreak
didn't seem
like an inevitable end
to every road

-heartbreak roads

how is it so easy for you
my dear
to make melodies
out of pain?

-melodies

you don't owe anyone
your time

-you belong to yourself

i want to give
my love
to someone
who deserves it
and love them
the way i wish
i had been loved
by everyone
who came before

-love given

it is not easy for me
to admit
that after everything
that happened
between us

i still
can't let go
of you

-can't let go

i thought that perhaps
after all this time
the cosmos was done
with bringing us together

but fate
has a funny way
of changing
when you least expect it

-the cosmos and us

i wanted to accept
your apology
far more
than you wanted
to give it

-apologies

i hate the way
i'm so desperate
to love you

-*desperate*

maybe
our ending
doesn't have to be
painful

-endings

sometimes it seems
like even love
couldn't piece my heart
back together
again

-*broken*

when someone hurts you
they don't get
to say
that they didn't

-hurt

i wish
i could have gotten
a clear answer
one way or another

-do you still love me?

i don't know
which part of me
wants you to stay
more

my body
or my heart

-body and heart

never let anyone
tell you
you are hard
to love

-abuse

mistakes
pushed us
apart

but fate
would not let us fall apart
so easily

-back together

Made in the USA
San Bernardino, CA
11 December 2019

61282100R00071